OFFICIAL SQA PAST PAPERS WITH ANSWERS

STANDARD GRADE | GENERAL

PHYSICS
2006-2009

© Scottish Qualifications Authority
All rights reserved. Copying prohibited. No part of this publication may be reproduced, stored in a retrieval system, or transmitted in any form or by any means, electronic, mechanical, photocopying, recording or otherwise.

First exam published in 2006.
Published by Bright Red Publishing Ltd, 6 Stafford Street, Edinburgh EH3 7AU
tel: 0131 220 5804 fax: 0131 220 6710 info@brightredpublishing.co.uk www.brightredpublishing.co.uk

ISBN 978-1-84948-023-9

A CIP Catalogue record for this book is available from the British Library.

Bright Red Publishing is grateful to the copyright holders, as credited on the final page of the book, for permission to use their material.
Every effort has been made to trace the copyright holders and to obtain their permission for the use of copyright material.
Bright Red Publishing will be happy to receive information allowing us to rectify any error or omission in future editions.

STANDARD GRADE | GENERAL

2006

[BLANK PAGE]

FOR OFFICIAL USE

G

K & U	PS

Total Marks

3220/401

NATIONAL
QUALIFICATIONS
2006

WEDNESDAY, 17 MAY
9.00 AM – 10.30 AM

PHYSICS
STANDARD GRADE
General Level

Fill in these boxes and read what is printed below.

Full name of centre

Town

Forename(s)

Surname

Date of birth
Day Month Year

Scottish candidate number

Number of seat

Reference may be made to the Physics Data Booklet.

1 All questions should be answered.

2 The questions may be answered in any order but all answers must be written clearly and legibly in this book.

3 For questions 1–7, write down, in the space provided, the letter corresponding to the answer you think is correct. There is only **one** correct answer.

4 For questions 8–19, write your answer where indicated by the question or in the space provided after the question.

5 If you change your mind about your answer you may score it out and replace it in the space provided at the end of the answer book.

6 Before leaving the examination room you must give this book to the invigilator. If you do not, you may lose all the marks for this paper.

SCOTTISH
QUALIFICATIONS
AUTHORITY

Marks

1. Which part of a television receiver picks up all signals?

   A   Tuner

   B   Modulator

   C   Decoder

   D   Amplifier

   E   Aerial

   Answer ☐   **1**

2. The nucleus of a uranium atom contains

   A   electrons only

   B   neutrons only

   C   electrons and protons only

   D   protons and neutrons only

   E   electrons, protons and neutrons.

   Answer ☐   **1**

3. What is the unit of equivalent dose?

   A   becquerel

   B   joule

   C   kilogram

   D   sievert

   E   watt

   Answer ☐   **1**

Marks

4. An uncharged capacitor C is connected to a resistor R, a 9 volt battery and a switch S as shown.

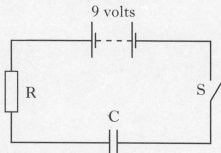

When switch S is closed the voltage across the capacitor

A   remains at 0 volt

B   gradually rises from 0 volt to 9 volts

C   immediately drops from 9 volts to 0 volt

D   gradually drops from 9 volts to 0 volt

E   remains at 9 volts.

Answer ☐   1

5. Which of the following is a unit of heat?

A   degree celsius

B   joule

C   joule per kilogram

D   joule per kilogram per degree celsius

E   watt

Answer ☐   1

6. Which of the following is the shortest distance?

The distance from the Earth to the

A   nearest star in our galaxy

B   edge of our galaxy

C   Moon

D   Sun

E   nearest planet.

Answer ☐   1

DO NOT WRITE IN THIS MARGIN

K&U	PS

Marks

7. Radio waves from space can be detected by a

A Geiger-Müller tube

B photographic plate

C scintillation counter

D telescope

E tuner.

Answer ☐ **1**

Marks

8. A factory chimney is demolished using explosives.

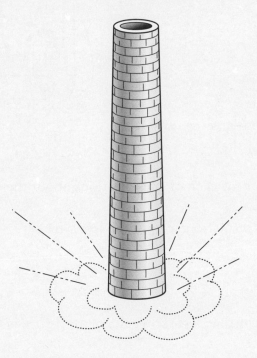

A crowd of people watches from a safe distance. A person in the crowd hears the sound 2·5 seconds after seeing the explosion.

(*a*) Explain why there is a delay between seeing the explosion and hearing the sound.

....

.... **1**

(*b*) Calculate the distance between the chimney and the person in the crowd. (The speed of sound in air is 340 metres per second.)

Space for working and answer

2

(*c*) Why should the demolition worker who sets off the explosives wear ear protectors to reduce the noise level to below 80 decibels?

....

....

.... **2**

Marks

9. The flex of a mains appliance has a 3-pin plug fitted as shown.

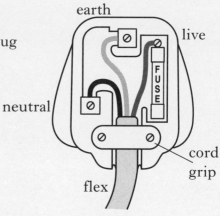

The flex contains three wires—live, neutral and earth.

(a) Circle the correct answer for each of the questions about the wires.

   (i) The colour of the insulation around the live wire is

$$\left\{\begin{array}{l}\text{blue}\\\text{brown}\\\text{green/yellow}\end{array}\right\}.$$

1

   (ii) The colour of the insulation around the neutral wire is

$$\left\{\begin{array}{l}\text{blue}\\\text{brown}\\\text{green/yellow}\end{array}\right\}.$$

1

   (iii) The $\left\{\begin{array}{l}\text{earth}\\\text{live}\\\text{neutral}\end{array}\right\}$ wire is a safety device.

1

(b) **Explain** why the flex must be held in place by the cord grip.

....

....

....

2

(c) Another appliance has only two wires in its flex. This appliance carries the following symbol.

   (i) Name this symbol.

....

1

   (ii) Which wire is not needed in this flex?

....

1

K&U   PS

Marks

10.   Read the following passage.

The temperature of the human body is maintained at about 37 degrees celsius. An increase or a decrease in body temperature of as little as 5 degrees celsius can be very serious.

Doctors often use ear thermometers to measure body temperature. Ear thermometers measure the infrared radiation emitted from the eardrum and surrounding tissue.

One type of ear thermometer has a scale that ranges from 32 degrees celsius to 42 degrees celsius. The temperature sensor used in this thermometer is a device that has a resistance which changes as the temperature changes.

Use information **given in the passage** to answer the following questions.

(a)   Name the type of radiation given out by the human body.

....   1

(b)   Give a reason why the scale of the ear thermometer ranges from 32 degrees celsius to 42 degrees celsius only.

....

....   1

(c)   Suggest a temperature sensor that could be used in the ear thermometer.

....   1

[Turn over

Marks

11. A student has a sight defect and is unable to see near objects clearly.

(*a*) The following diagram shows what happens to light rays when the student is reading a book.

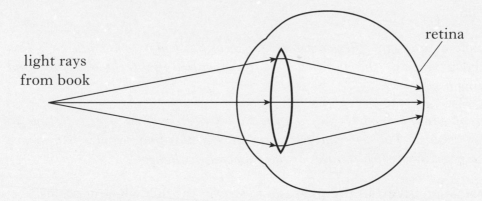

(i) By referring to the diagram, explain why the student sees a blurred image.

....

.... **1**

(ii) Name this sight defect.

.... **1**

(iii) In the space below, draw the shape of the lens that would correct this sight defect.

Space for diagram

1

(iv) When this sight defect has been corrected, the student looks at a picture printed in the book.

Which statement describes the image on the retina of the student's eye compared to the actual picture?

A The image is the same way up and larger.

B The image is upside down and larger.

C The image is the same way up and smaller.

D The image is upside down and smaller.

Answer **1**

Marks

11. (continued)

(*b*) Another student has a different eye defect. This student is prescribed spectacles that have red tinted glass. The graph below shows the percentage of light of different colours that passes through this glass.

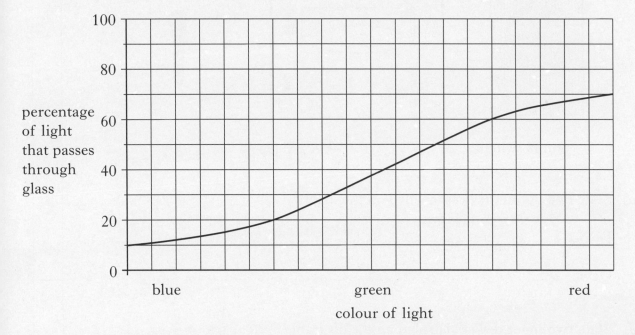

(i) Which colour of light is blocked most by the tinted glass?

.... 1

(ii) List the three colours given on the graph in order of **decreasing** wavelength.

.... 1

[Turn over

Marks

12. A karaoke machine contains various input and output devices.

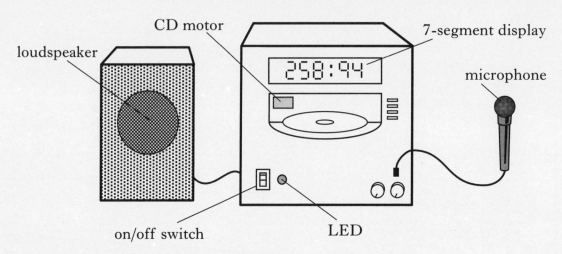

(*a*) State **two** output devices labelled on the diagram.

Device 1 ....

Device 2   2

(*b*) State **two** input devices labelled on the diagram.

Device 1 ....

Device 2   2

(*c*) The karaoke machine has an LED.

(i) State the useful energy transfer that takes place in the LED.

.... to   1

(ii) In the space below draw the symbol for an LED.

Space for symbol

1

Marks

13. A technician uses a signal generator and two oscilloscopes as shown to test an amplifier.

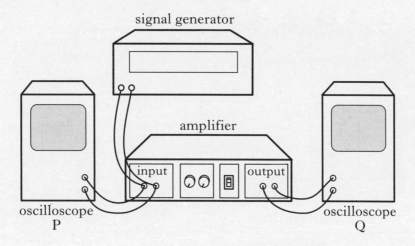

(a) The screens of both oscilloscopes are shown below.

input signal to amplifier

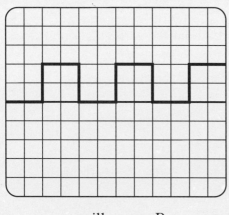

oscilloscope P

output signal from amplifier

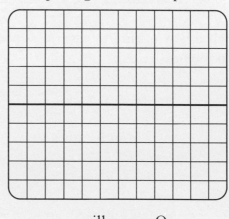

oscilloscope Q

The settings on both oscilloscopes are identical.

(i) Complete the diagram to show the amplified output signal seen on oscilloscope Q.   **2**

(ii) Circle the correct answer in the statement below.

The signal shown on oscilloscope P is $\left\{ \begin{array}{l} \text{analogue} \\ \text{decimal} \\ \text{digital} \end{array} \right\}$.   **1**

(b) Which of the following devices contains an amplifier?

lamp   **radio**   **relay**   **transformer**

....   **1**

Marks

14. A rowing crew takes part in a race.

The time for their boat at each stage of the race is shown.

		Time from start	
		minutes	*seconds*
Start:	0 metres	00	00
	500 metres	01	40
	1000 metres	03	50
	1500 metres	05	50
Finish:	2000 metres	07	45

(*a*) **Describe** how to find the average speed of the boat from the start of the race to the finish.

....

....

....

....

....   **3**

(*b*) Calculate the average speed of the boat during the first 500 metres of the race.

Space for working and answer

2

Marks

14. (continued)

(*c*) The crew supplies a force to move the boat forward. When the boat is moving, a force opposes the motion of the boat.

   (i) Name the force that opposes the motion of the boat.

.... 1

   (ii) During the first 500 metres, there is a constant unbalanced force acting on the boat.

Describe the motion of the boat during this section of the race.

.... 1

   (iii) During one stage of the race, the speed of the boat is constant.

What can be said about the forces acting on the boat during this stage?

.... 1

[Turn over

Marks

15. A car is being repaired in a garage. The car is on a ramp and is raised to a height of 1·5 metres.

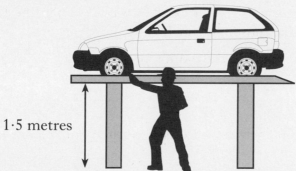

1·5 metres

The car has a mass of 1200 kilograms.

(a) Calculate the weight of the car.

Space for working and answer

2

(b) Calculate how much gravitational potential energy the car has gained when it is 1·5 metres above the garage floor.

Space for working and answer

2

(c) The car is raised in 12 seconds.

(i) Calculate the minimum power needed to lift the car 1·5 metres in 12 seconds.

Space for working and answer

2

(ii) In practice, the power needed to raise the car in this time is greater than the minimum power.

Explain why.

....

.... 1

Marks

16. A fan operates using a solar cell and a light bulb.

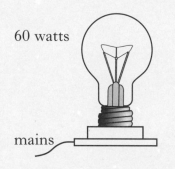
60 watts

mains

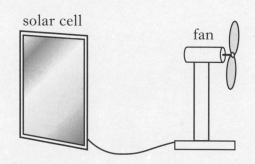
solar cell   fan

(*a*) What energy transformation takes place in the **solar cell**?

.... to **1**

(*b*) When the lamp is on, the fan turns slowly.

(i) Suggest **two** changes that could be made which would make the fan turn faster.

Change 1 ....

Change 2 .... **2**

(ii) The 60 watt lamp operates for 2 minutes.

Calculate how much energy is transformed by the lamp in this time.

Space for working and answer

2

(*c*) Solar energy is a renewable source of energy.

(i) Name **one** other renewable source of energy.

.... **1**

(ii) Name a non-renewable source of energy.

.... **1**

[Turn over

Marks

17. The diagram shows all the ways in which heat is lost from a house.

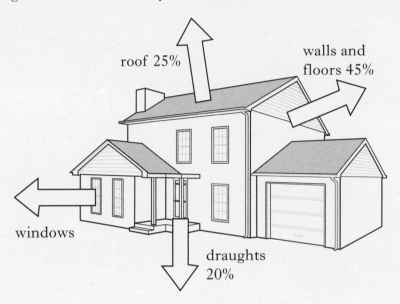

roof 25%

walls and floors 45%

windows

draughts 20%

(a) Using information from the diagram, calculate the percentage of heat lost through windows.

Space for working and answer

2

(b) Various windows of area one square metre are tested for rate of heat loss. The results are shown in the table.

Window	Rate of heat loss (joules per second)
single glazed	80
double glazed	60
triple glazed	50

(i) How many joules of heat are lost per square metre from a single glazed window every second?

....   1

Marks

17. (*b*) (continued)

(ii) All the windows in a particular house are single glazed. Every second a total of 500 joules of heat is lost through the windows in this house.

(A) Calculate the total area of the windows.

> *Space for working and answer*

2

(B) Describe **one** way of reducing heat loss through the windows in this house.

....

.... **1**

(*c*) A householder keeps the temperature in a house at 20 degrees celsius all year.

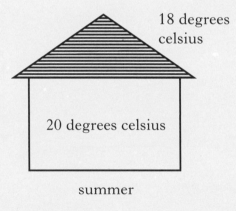

18 degrees celsius

20 degrees celsius

summer

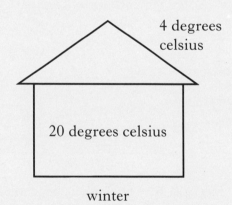

4 degrees celsius

20 degrees celsius

winter

At which time of the year is the rate of heat loss from this house greater? Explain your answer.

....

....

.... **2**

Marks

18. A 5 volt battery in a mobile phone is recharged from the mains using a charger containing a step down transformer.

(*a*) The transformer consists of three parts.

core   primary coil   secondary coil

Label each of these parts on the diagram below.

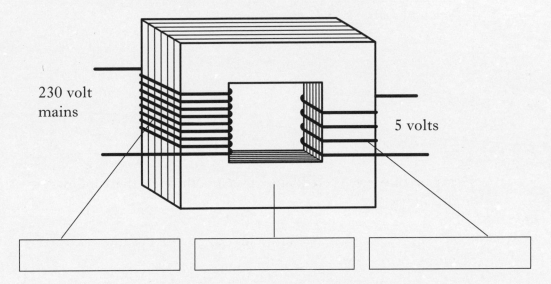

230 volt
mains

5 volts

3

(*b*) There are 11 500 turns on the primary coil of the transformer.

Calculate the number of turns on the secondary coil.

Space for working and answer

2

(*c*) **Explain** why a transformer cannot be used to step down the voltage from a battery.

....

....

.... 2

Marks

19. A spacecraft is far out in space. An astronaut wearing a backpack leaves the spacecraft. The astronaut uses the backpack to move around. The backpack contains a pressurised gas cylinder connected to a valve. When the valve is opened, a jet of gas is released.

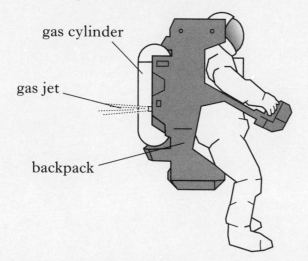

gas cylinder

gas jet

backpack

(a) Complete the passage below by circling the correct answer.

When the astronaut opens the valve, the cylinder pushes gas backwards.

The gas pushes the $\begin{cases} \text{cylinder} \\ \text{jet} \\ \text{spacecraft} \end{cases}$ forwards.

1

(b) The astronaut and backpack have a combined mass of 120 kilograms. The jet of gas exerts a constant thrust of 24 newtons.

(i) Calculate the acceleration of the astronaut when the jet is switched on.

> *Space for working and answer*

2

(ii) The jet is now switched off.

Describe the motion of the astronaut.

Explain your answer.

....

....

....

2

[END OF QUESTION PAPER]

YOU MAY USE THE SPACE ON THIS PAGE TO REWRITE ANY ANSWER YOU HAVE DECIDED TO CHANGE IN THE MAIN PART OF THE ANSWER BOOKLET. TAKE CARE TO WRITE IN CAREFULLY THE APPROPRIATE QUESTION NUMBER.

STANDARD GRADE | GENERAL

2007

[BLANK PAGE]

G

FOR OFFICIAL USE

K & U	PS

Total Marks

3220/401

NATIONAL
QUALIFICATIONS
2007

WEDNESDAY, 16 MAY
9.00 AM – 10.30 AM

PHYSICS
STANDARD GRADE
General Level

Fill in these boxes and read what is printed below.

Full name of centre

Town

Forename(s)

Surname

Date of birth

Day Month Year   Scottish candidate number   Number of seat

Reference may be made to the Physics Data Booklet.

1 All questions should be answered.

2 The questions may be answered in any order but all answers must be written clearly and legibly in this book.

3 For questions 1–5, write down, in the space provided, the letter corresponding to the answer you think is correct. There is only **one** correct answer.

4 For questions 6–18, write your answer where indicated by the question or in the space provided after the question.

5 If you change your mind about your answer you may score it out and replace it in the space provided at the end of the answer book.

6 Before leaving the examination room you must give this book to the invigilator. If you do not, you may lose all the marks for this paper.

SCOTTISH
QUALIFICATIONS
AUTHORITY

©

Marks

1. Which part of a radio receiver separates the audio signal from the carrier wave?

    A   Aerial

    B   Tuner

    C   Decoder

    D   Amplifier

    E   Loudspeaker

    Answer ☐   **1**

2. Four **identical** resistors, P, Q, R and S are connected as shown.

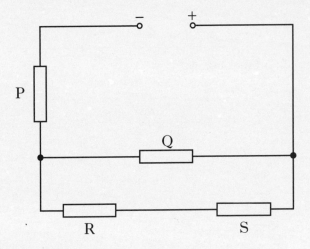

    In which of the resistors is the current the same?

    A   P and Q only

    B   R and S only

    C   P, R and S only

    D   Q, R and S only

    E   P, Q, R and S.

    Answer ☐   **1**

Marks

3. Which row of values would result in the greatest kinetic energy?

	Mass (kilograms)	Speed (metres per second)
A	45	8
B	45	4
C	50	10
D	50	8
E	50	4

Answer ☐   1

4. A rocket is pushed forwards because its engine gases

    A   are pushed backwards

    B   spread outwards

    C   are pushed forwards

    D   surround the rocket

    E   spread inwards.

Answer ☐   1

5. In outer space, the engine of a space probe is switched on for a short time. When the engine is switched off, the rocket

    A   changes direction

    B   moves at a steady speed

    C   slows down

    D   speeds up

    E   follows a curved path.

Answer ☐   1

[Turn over

Marks

6. A surfer rides the waves near a beach.

(a) The diagram below shows a wave some distance from the beach.

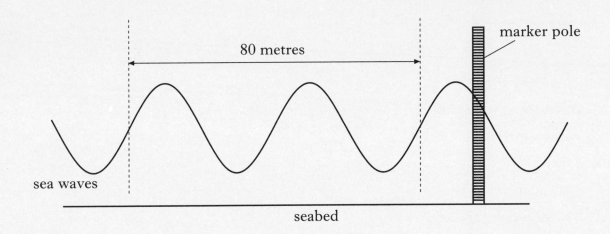

(i) Using information from the diagram, calculate the wavelength of the wave.

> *Space for working and answer*

2

(ii) The time between one crest and the next crest passing the marker pole is 5 seconds.

Calculate the speed of the wave.

> *Space for working and answer*

2

Marks

6. (a) (continued)

    (iii) Calculate the frequency of the wave.

        Space for working and answer

        2

(b) The drawing below shows changes in the wave as it approaches the beach.

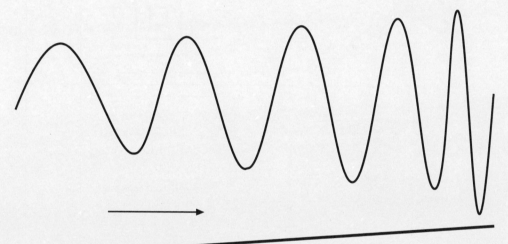

seabed

Complete the sentences below by circling the correct answers.

    (i) As the wave approaches the beach,

        its wavelength $\begin{cases} \text{decreases} \\ \text{increases} \\ \text{stays the same} \end{cases}$.   **1**

    (ii) As the wave approaches the beach,

        its amplitude $\begin{cases} \text{decreases} \\ \text{increases} \\ \text{stays the same} \end{cases}$.   **1**

[Turn over

Marks

7. Appliances convert electrical energy into other forms of energy.

Appliance	*Rating plate*
Food processor	230 volts 50 hertz 400 watts
Hair dryer	230 volts 50 hertz □ 1200 watts
Kettle	230 volts 50 hertz 2200 watts
Lamp	230 volts 50 hertz □ 60 watts

(*a*) State the **useful** energy output from the following appliances.

    (i) Lamp: electrical energy ⟶ .... energy   **1**

    (ii) Kettle: electrical energy ⟶ .... energy   **1**

7. (continued)

(b)   (i)   Name **one** appliance from the table which requires an earth wire.

....   1

(ii)   Circle **one** word or phrase in the passage below to make the statement correct.

The colouring of the insulation around the earth wire is

$\left\{ \begin{array}{l} \text{blue} \\ \text{brown} \\ \text{green and yellow} \end{array} \right\}$.   1

(iii)   Each appliance is fitted with either a 3 ampere or 13 ampere fuse. State the correct value of fuse for the following appliances.

(A)   Lamp:...   1

(B)   Hair dryer:...   1

[Turn over

Marks

8. A mobile phone contains a battery which is charged using a base unit. The base unit contains a transformer and is connected to the a.c. mains supply.

mobile phone
containing battery

base unit containing
transformer

to a.c. mains supply

(a) What is the purpose of the mains supply?

.... **1**

(b) Name the supply mentioned which is d.c.

.... **1**

(c) a.c. is short for alternating current.
Explain what is meant by alternating current.

....

.... **1**

(d) State the purpose of a transformer.

....

.... **1**

(e) State **one** advantage of using a mobile phone.

....

.... **1**

9. One of the spotlights on a stage does not work. A continuity tester is used to find the fault. The continuity tester contains a lamp and a 1·5 volt battery.

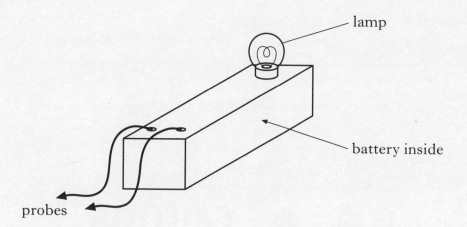

(a) Complete the circuit diagram for the continuity tester.
You must use the correct symbols for all components.

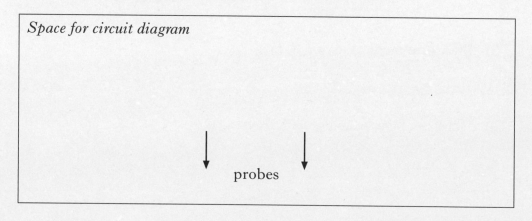

3

(b) Describe how you could check that the continuity tester is working properly.

....

.... **2**

(c) The continuity tester shows that the fault in the spotlight is an open circuit.
What is meant by an open circuit?

.... **1**

[Turn over

DO NOT
WRITE IN
THIS
MARGIN

K&U | PS

Marks

10.   Different types of radiation are used to detect and treat illnesses and injuries. Four of these radiations are

| infrared | laser light | ultraviolet | X-rays |

(a)   What type of radiation is used to treat skin conditions such as acne?

....   1

(b)

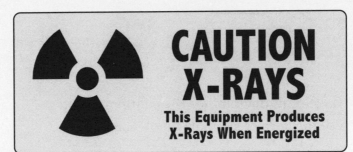

(i)   State **one** medical use of X-rays.

....   1

(ii)   What can be used to detect X-rays?

....   1

Marks

10.   (continued)

(*c*)

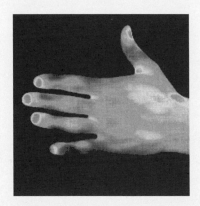

Colour photographs called thermograms are used to find the temperature variation in a patient's body.

Name the radiation used to make thermograms.

....   1

(*d*)

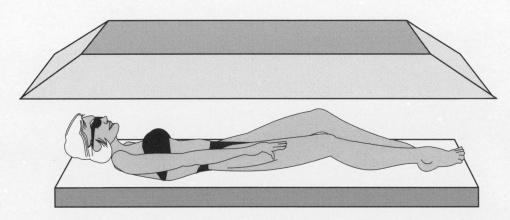

Explain why people need to be protected from overexposure to ultraviolet radiation.

....   1

[Turn over

K&U | PS

Marks

11. A class investigates the effects of the following shapes of glass on rays of white light.

The teacher sets up three experiments, covering the glass shape with card. The paths of the light rays entering and leaving the different shapes of glass are shown.

For each of the three experiments, draw the **shape** and **position** of the glass block that was used.

(*a*)

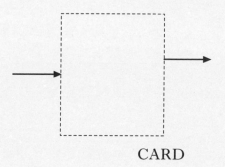

CARD

2

(*b*)

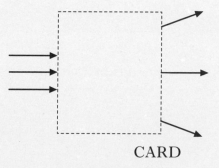

CARD

2

(*c*)

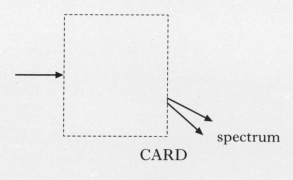

spectrum

CARD

2

Marks

12. A radio and a computer mouse are examples of electronic systems.

(*a*) An electronic system can be represented by a block diagram as shown. Complete the block diagram by filling in the missing labels.

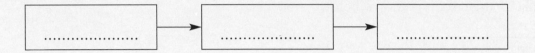

3

(*b*) Output signals from an electronic system can be either analogue or digital.

(i) The output signal from a radio is analogue.

Draw an analogue signal.

> *Space for drawing*

1

(ii) The output signal from a computer mouse is digital.

Draw a digital signal.

> *Space for drawing*

1

Marks

13. An electronic system is used to control a lift. When a floor has been selected, two checks are made:

there are no obstructions to the doors;
the lift is not overloaded.

Part of the circuit is shown below.

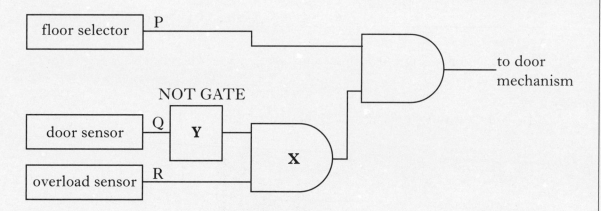

The logic states are as shown for the floor selector, the sensors and the door mechanism.

		logic level
floor selector	not pressed	0
	pressed	1
door sensor	no obstruction	0
	obstruction	1
overload sensor	overloaded	0
	not overloaded	1
door mechanism	doors open	0
	doors closed	1

(a) Name logic gate **X**.

....   **1**

Marks

13. (continued)

(b) (i) Gate **Y** is a NOT gate.

Draw the symbol for a NOT gate.

Space for symbol

1

(ii) Complete the truth table for a NOT gate.

Input	Output
0	
1	

1

(c) (i) State the logic levels needed at P, Q and R to close the lift doors.

Logic level at P ....

Logic level at Q ....

Logic level at R ....

3

(ii) What output device could be used for the door opening and closing mechanism?

....

1

[Turn over

Marks

14. In a tennis match, the player hits the ball to serve.

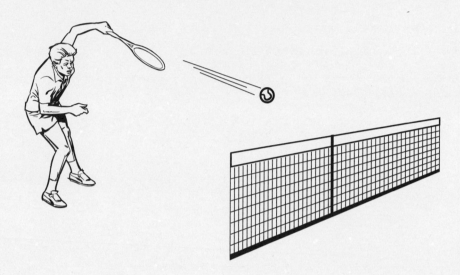

(*a*) The ball travels 24 metres from the server's racquet to the opponent's racquet at an average speed of 40 metres per second.

Calculate the time taken.

Space for working and answer

2

Marks

14. **(continued)**

(b) A graph showing how the speed of the ball changes while in contact with the racquet during the serve is shown.

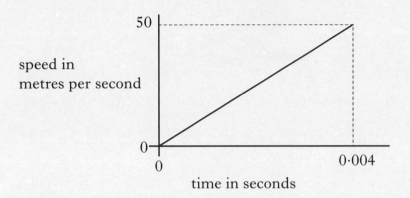

Calculate the acceleration of the ball during the serve.

Space for working and answer

2

(c) For a second serve, the server hits the ball with a smaller force.

What effect does this have on the speed of the ball when it leaves the racquet?

....

1

[Turn over

K&U PS

Marks

15. A skier takes part in a downhill competition.

(*a*) State **two** ways the skier can reduce friction in order to reach high speeds.

....

.... 2

(*b*) When the skier reaches the maximum speed of 65 metres per second, this speed is maintained over the rest of the course.

State how the size of the downhill force compares with the size of the frictional force during this part of the course.

.... 1

(*c*) At the end of the course, the frictional force brings the skier to rest over a horizontal distance of 500 metres. During this distance, the average frictional force is 346 newtons.

Calculate the work done to bring the skier to rest.

Space for working and answer

2

Marks

16. A student carries out an experiment to find out which mug is the best at keeping drinks hot.

Each mug is made from a different material.

plastic

metal

ceramic

The same volume of hot water is added to each mug.

(*a*) Describe how the student could carry out the experiment.
Your description should include:

> what apparatus would be used;
> what measurements are made;
> how you reach a conclusion.

....

....

....

....

....

....   **3**

(*b*) How could the heat lost from the mugs be reduced?

....   **1**

[Turn over

K&U | PS

Marks

17. A householder installs a wind turbine electricity generator.

The table gives information about the wind turbine.

Rated power output	1·5 kilowatts
Product life	20 years
Installation cost	£1600

(*a*) In the year 2006, the wind turbine generated electricity for 2000 hours. Calculate the energy generated in kilowatt-hours during 2006.

Space for working and answer

2

DO NOT WRITE IN THIS MARGIN

K&U PS

Marks

17. (continued)

(*b*) An electricity supplier charges 8 pence per kilowatt-hour.

Calculate the cost of buying the same amount of electricity as generated by the wind turbine in 2006.

Space for working and answer

2

(*c*) The wind turbine costs £1600 to install. It is used to generate energy for 20 years. Each year it generates the same amount of energy as it did in 2006.

Calculate how much money the householder will save if the turbine is used to generate electricity over this time.

Space for working and answer

2

[Turn over

K&U PS

Marks

18. The diagram below shows a refracting telescope, which is used by astronomers to view distant stars, planets and galaxies.

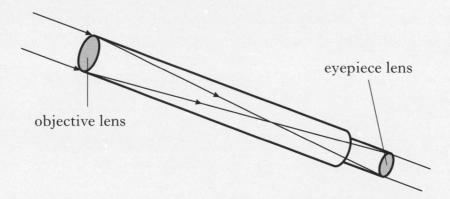

eyepiece lens

objective lens

(*a*) (i) Which lens, the objective or the eyepiece, has the longer focal length?

.... **1**

(ii) What is the purpose of the eyepiece lens?

.... **1**

Marks

18. (continued)

(b) The table gives information about some of the planets in our Solar System.

Planet	Diameter (kilometres)	Distance from Sun (million kilometres)	Weight of one kilogram at surface (newtons)	Time to go around the Sun once (years)	Time for one complete spin (in Earth days or hours)
Mercury	4800	58	4	0·25	59 days
Venus	12 000	110	9	0·6	243 days
Earth	12 750	150	10	1	24 hours
Mars	7000	228	4	1·9	25 hours
Jupiter	140 000	780	26	12	10 hours
Saturn	120 000	1430	11	30	10 hours
Neptune	50 000	4500	12	165	16 hours

(i) Which planet has the longest day?

.... 1

(ii) Which planet has the longest orbit?

.... 1

(iii) On which planet would a 4 kilogram mass have the greatest weight?

.... 1

(c) A meteorite is the name given to an object which enters the Earth's atmosphere from space. When they enter the atmosphere, meteorites heat up.

State the energy change when the meteorite enters the atmosphere.

.... 1

(d) Stars and planets belong to galaxies.
What is a galaxy?

.... 1

[END OF QUESTION PAPER]

YOU MAY USE THE SPACE ON THIS PAGE TO REWRITE ANY ANSWER YOU HAVE DECIDED TO CHANGE IN THE MAIN PART OF THE ANSWER BOOKLET. TAKE CARE TO WRITE IN CAREFULLY THE APPROPRIATE QUESTION NUMBER.

YOU MAY USE THE SPACE ON THIS PAGE TO REWRITE ANY ANSWER YOU HAVE DECIDED TO CHANGE IN THE MAIN PART OF THE ANSWER BOOKLET. TAKE CARE TO WRITE IN CAREFULLY THE APPROPRIATE QUESTION NUMBER.

YOU MAY USE THE SPACE ON THIS PAGE TO REWRITE ANY ANSWER YOU HAVE DECIDED TO CHANGE IN THE MAIN PART OF THE ANSWER BOOKLET. TAKE CARE TO WRITE IN CAREFULLY THE APPROPRIATE QUESTION NUMBER.

**YOU MAY USE THE SPACE ON THIS PAGE TO REWRITE ANY ANSWER
YOU HAVE DECIDED TO CHANGE IN THE MAIN PART OF THE ANSWER
BOOKLET. TAKE CARE TO WRITE IN CAREFULLY THE APPROPRIATE
QUESTION NUMBER.**

[BLANK PAGE]

STANDARD GRADE | GENERAL

2008

[BLANK PAGE]

FOR OFFICIAL USE

G

K & U	PS

Total Marks

3220/401

NATIONAL
QUALIFICATIONS
2008

FRIDAY, 23 MAY
9.00 AM – 10.30 AM

PHYSICS
STANDARD GRADE
General Level

Fill in these boxes and read what is printed below.

Full name of centre

Town

Forename(s)

Surname

Date of birth
Day Month Year

Scottish candidate number

Number of seat

Reference may be made to the Physics Data Booklet.

1 All questions should be answered.

2 The questions may be answered in any order but all answers must be written clearly and legibly in this book.

3 For questions 1–5, write down, in the space provided, the letter corresponding to the answer you think is correct. There is only **one** correct answer.

4 For questions 6–20, write your answer where indicated by the question or in the space provided after the question.

5 If you change your mind about your answer you may score it out and replace it in the space provided at the end of the answer book.

6 Before leaving the examination room you must give this book to the invigilator. If you do not, you may lose all the marks for this paper.

Marks

1. When a student whistles a note into a microphone connected to an oscilloscope, the following pattern is displayed.

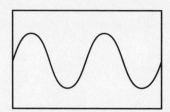

Without changing the oscilloscope controls, another student whistles a quieter note of higher frequency into the microphone. Which of the following shows the pattern which would be displayed on the screen?

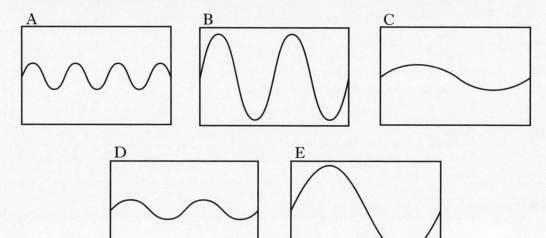

Answer ☐   1

2. The weather information satellite NOAA-15 has a period of 99 minutes and an orbital height of 833 kilometres.

The geostationary weather information satellite Meteosat has a period of 1440 minutes and an orbital height of 35 900 kilometres.

Which of the following gives the period of a satellite that has an orbital height of 20 000 kilometres?

A   83 minutes

B   99 minutes

C   720 minutes

D   1440 minutes

E   1750 minutes

Answer ☐   1

Marks

3. Which row in the table describes the correct configuration for an atom?

	orbiting the nucleus	*inside the nucleus*
A	protons only	electrons and neutrons
B	electrons and protons	neutrons only
C	neutrons and protons	electrons only
D	electrons only	neutrons and protons
E	neutrons only	electrons and protons

Answer ☐   **1**

4. The time taken for light to reach us from the Sun is approximately

A   1 second

B   8 seconds

C   1 minute

D   8 minutes

E   1 hour.

Answer ☐   **1**

5. Two objects are dropped from the same height. Both objects fall freely.

Object X has a mass of 10 kilograms.

Object Y has a mass of 1 kilogram.

Object X accelerates at 10 metres per second per second.

The acceleration of object Y, in metres per second per second, is

A   0·1

B   1·0

C   10

D   100

E   1000.

Answer ☐   **1**

[Turn over

Marks

6. A student is listening to a radio.

(a) Complete the passage below using words from the following list.

sound	**amplifier**	**light**	**microphone**
aerial	**battery**	**tuner**	**decoder**	**electrical**

The .... of a radio receiver detects signals from many different stations and converts them into electrical signals.

The .... selects one particular station from many.

The .... increases the amplitude of these electrical signals.

The energy required to do this is supplied by the ....

The loudspeaker in a radio receiver converts .... energy into

.... energy.

3

DO NOT
WRITE IN
THIS
MARGIN

K&U   PS

Marks

6. **(continued)**

(*b*) Electrical signals are displayed as waves on an oscilloscope.

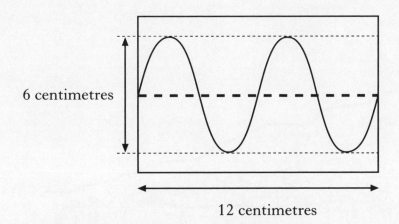

6 centimetres

12 centimetres

(i) Calculate the wavelength of the waves.

Space for working and answer

1

(ii) Calculate the amplitude of the waves.

Space for working and answer

1

[Turn over

Marks

7. A football match is being broadcast live from Dundee. Signals from the football stadium are transmitted to a television studio in Glasgow via a relay station on top of a nearby hill.

At the relay station, a curved reflector is placed behind a detector of the television signals.

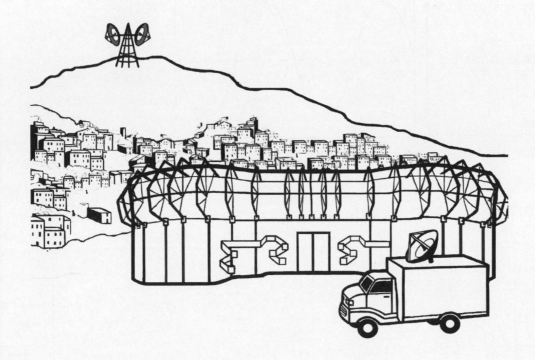

(*a*) (i) State the purpose of the curved reflector.

....   1

(ii) Complete the diagram below to show the effect of the curved reflector on the signal at the relay station.

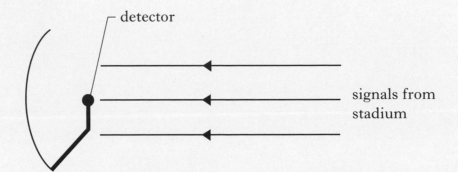

2

K&U | PS

Marks

7. (continued)

(*b*) During the match, strong winds cause the reflector to move to a new position as shown.

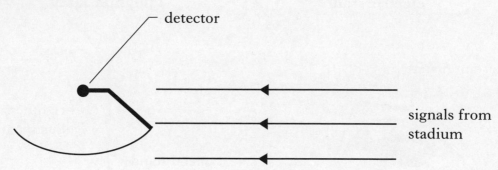

State the effect this has on the signal received at the detector.

.... **1**

[Turn over

Marks

8. Two household electrical appliances, a 1500 watt electric iron and a 300 watt uplighter lamp, are shown below.

electric iron

uplighter lamp

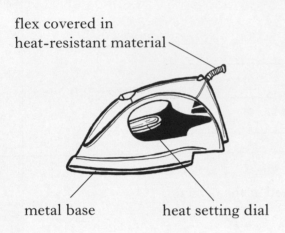

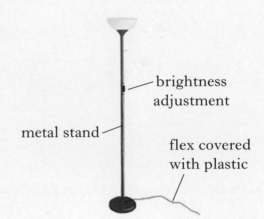

flex covered in
heat-resistant material

metal base   heat setting dial

brightness
adjustment

metal stand

flex covered
with plastic

(a) The brightness of the uplighter lamp can be changed.

State an electrical component that could be used to change the brightness of the uplighter lamp.

....   1

(b) Explain why the flex for the iron is covered with a heat-resistant material.

....   1

Marks

8. **(continued)**

(*c*) A cross-section of the flex for each appliance is shown.

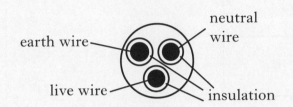

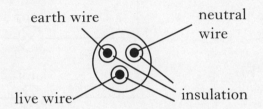

electric iron   uplighter lamp

(i)   State the colour of the insulation on the live wire.

.... 1

(ii) State the purpose of the earth wire.

.... 1

(iii) Explain why the wires in the flex for the electric iron are thicker than those for the uplighter lamp.

.... 1

[Turn over

9. Two identical lamps are connected to a 6·0 volt battery as shown in circuit 1.

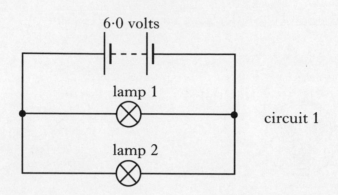

     circuit 1

(a) The battery supplies a current of 0·40 ampere to the circuit.

Complete the following table to show the current in each lamp and the voltage across each lamp.

	Lamp 1	Lamp 2
Current (amperes)		
Voltage (volts)		

2

(b) The two lamps are now connected as shown in circuit 2.

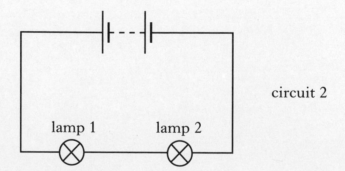

     circuit 2

State the voltage of the battery required to light the lamps with the same brightness as in circuit 1.

.... **1**

(c) In which of the two circuits, circuit 1 or circuit 2, would lamp 2 still be on when lamp 1 is removed?

.... **1**

Marks

10. (*a*) A drummer in a rock band is exposed to sound levels of up to 110 decibels.

Explain why ear protectors are used to reduce the sound level experienced by the drummer.

.... **1**

(*b*) A medical researcher is measuring the upper range of hearing of people in different age groups.

The bar graph shows the frequencies of sound detected by these people.

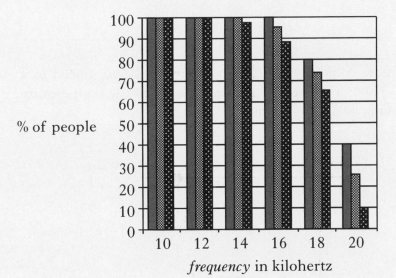

(i) State **two** conclusions which can be made from this bar graph about the hearing of different age groups.

....

.... **2**

(ii) What name is given to sound frequencies greater than 20 kilohertz?

.... **1**

K&U | PS

Marks

11. (*a*) A thermistor is connected to a 6·0 volt supply in circuit 1. The table gives some information about the thermistor.

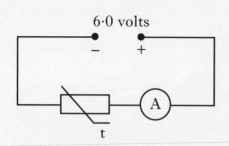

6·0 volts

circuit 1

temperature (degrees Celsius)	resistance (ohms)
20	1000
30	600
40	400

Calculate the reading on the ammeter when the thermistor is placed in a beaker of water at 40 degrees celsius.

Space for working and answer

3

(*b*) The thermistor is now connected as shown in circuit 2 and placed in a tropical fish tank. The circuit provides a warning when the temperature of the water in the tank becomes too low.

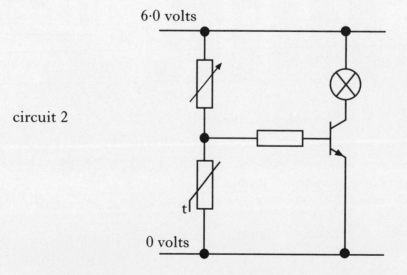

6·0 volts

circuit 2

0 volts

(i) What is the purpose of the transistor in circuit 2?

.... 1

Marks

K&U	PS

11. *(b)* **(continued)**

(ii) The same components are used to construct circuit 3.

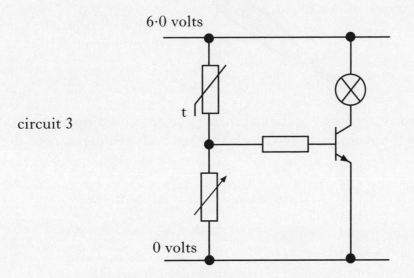

circuit 3

State how the operation of circuit 3 differs from the operation of circuit 2.

.... 1

[Turn over

K&U | PS

Marks

12. (*a*) A nurse uses a clinical thermometer to measure the body temperature of a patient. The temperature of the patient is 39 degrees celsius.

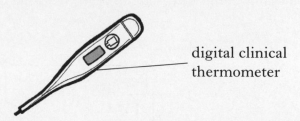
digital clinical thermometer

(i) Give **two** reasons why a clinical thermometer is used instead of an ordinary thermometer when measuring the body temperature of the patient.

....

.... **2**

(ii) Why does the nurse conclude that the patient is unwell?

.... **1**

(*b*) Radioactive sources are used in the treatment of many illnesses. The table below gives some properties of three radioactive sources used in medicine.

Name of Source	Type of Source	Half-life of Source
Radium – 226	Alpha	1600 years
Iodine – 131	Beta	8 days
Technetium – 99	Gamma	6 hours

(i) One type of treatment requires a source that produces high ionisation.
Which source should be used?

.... **1**

(ii) Which source would be most suitable for use in diagnostic tests where a tracer is injected into the body?

.... **1**

(iii) Which source should not be stored in an aluminium box for safety reasons?

.... **1**

Marks

13. An electronic system is designed to count the number of vehicles that enter a car park.

When a vehicle enters the car park it cuts through a beam of light and a sensor circuit produces a digital pulse. The number of pulses produced by the sensor circuit is then counted and decoded before being displayed. The display consists of a number of illuminated sections.

A diagram for part of this system is shown.

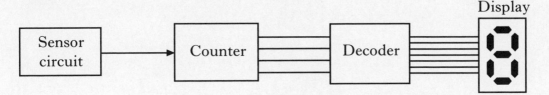

(a) (i) Select a suitable device **from the list below** to be used as an input for the sensor circuit.

    LDR   **thermistor**   **microphone**   **capacitor**

.... 1

(ii) Complete the sentence below by circling the correct answer.

The output of the counter is $\left\{ \begin{array}{l} \text{analogue} \\ \text{binary} \\ \text{decimal} \end{array} \right\}$.   1

(iii) Name the device used to display the number of vehicles that enter the car park.

.... 1

(b) The counter is reset to zero. Over a period of time, the sensor circuit then produces the following signal.

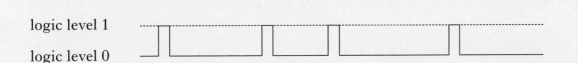

On the diagram of the display below, shade in the sections that should be illuminated to show the number of vehicles that have entered the car park during this time.

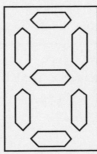

1

Marks

14. A walker wears a pedometer. A pedometer is an instrument that measures the distance walked by counting the number of steps taken. The walker measures the distance of one step as 0·8 metres, and enters it into the pedometer.

0·8 metres

(*a*) The walker completes 9000 steps during a walk.

Calculate the distance travelled.

> *Space for working and answer*

1

(*b*) The walker completes this walk in 80 minutes.

What is the average speed of the walker in **metres per second**?

> *Space for working and answer*

2

(*c*) Give a reason why the distance measured by the pedometer may not be accurate.

....

1

Marks

15. A piano of mass 250 kilograms is pushed up a ramp into a van by applying a constant force of 600 newtons as shown.

The ramp is 3 metres long and the van floor is 0·75 metres above the ground.

(*a*) (i) Calculate the weight of the piano.

> *Space for working and answer*

2

(ii) What is the minimum force required to lift the piano vertically into the van?

.... 1

(*b*) Calculate the work done pushing the piano up the ramp.

> *Space for working and answer*

2

(*c*) How can the force required to push the piano up the ramp be reduced?

.... 1

[Turn over

Marks

16. A traffic information sign is located in a remote area.

The sign is supplied with energy by both a panel of solar cells and a wind generator. The panel of solar cells and the wind generator are connected to a rechargeable battery.

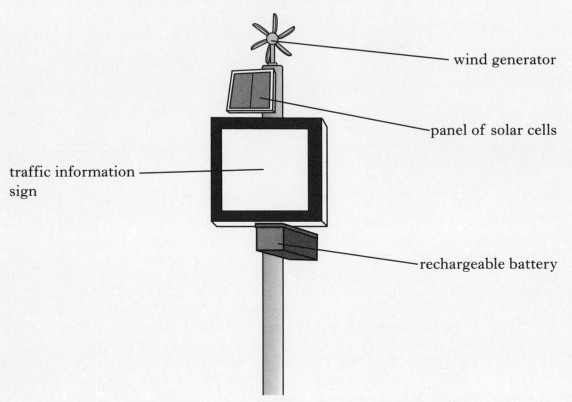

wind generator

panel of solar cells

traffic information sign

rechargeable battery

(a) One square metre of solar cells can generate up to 80 watts.
The panel of solar cells has an area of 0·4 square metres.

(i) State the energy change that takes place in the solar cells.

.... **1**

(ii) Calculate the maximum power produced by the panel of solar cells.

Space for working and answer

1

Marks

16. (continued)

(b) The following table shows the power produced by the wind generator at different wind speeds.

wind speed (metres per second)	power output of wind generator (watts)
2	8
4	16
6	
8	32
10	40

(i) Suggest the power produced when the wind speed is 6 metres per second.

....   **1**

(ii) At a wind speed of 10 metres per second the voltage produced by the wind generator is 16 volts.

Calculate the current produced by the wind generator.

Space for working and answer

2

(c) Explain why a rechargeable battery is also required to supply energy to the traffic information sign.

....   **1**

[Turn over

Marks

17. (*a*) A digital camera contains a rechargeable battery. The battery requires a voltage of 5·75 volts to be recharged. The battery is recharged using a transformer connected to the mains supply. The transformer is used to step down the 230 volt a.c. mains supply to 5·75 volts.

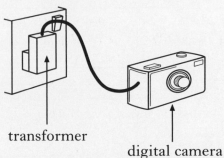

transformer

digital camera

The transformer has 2000 turns on the primary coil.

(i) Calculate the number of turns on the secondary coil.

> *Space for working and answer*

2

(ii) Give **one** reason why a transformer cannot be used to charge the camera battery from a 12 volt d.c. car battery.

....   1

(*b*) Complete the following passage.

In the National Grid, ... transformers are used to increase the 25 000 volts from a power station to 132 000 volts for transmission.

This reduces .... in the transmission lines.

The voltage is then decreased to 11 000 volts for industry and 230 volts

for domestic use using .... transformers.   3

Marks

18. A coolant pack is used to treat an injured player at a hockey match.

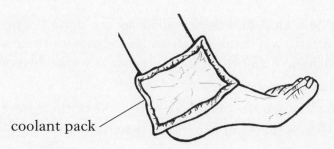

coolant pack

Before use the coolant pack is stored in a refrigerator at 2 degrees celsius.

The coolant inside the pack changes state from liquid to solid.

The coolant has a melting point of 7 degrees celsius and a mass of 0·5 kilograms.

The coolant pack is removed from the refrigerator and placed on the injured ankle of a player.

(*a*) (i) Calculate the energy required to raise the temperature of the coolant pack from 2 degrees celsius to its melting point.

(specific heat capacity of coolant = 2100 joules per kilogram per degree celsius)

Space for working and answer

3

(ii) Where does most of the energy required to raise the temperature of the coolant pack come from?

.... 1

(*b*) Having reached its melting point the coolant pack then remains at the same temperature for 15 minutes.

What is happening to the coolant during this time?

.... 1

(*c*) One of the other players suggests insulating the coolant pack and ankle with a towel.

Why should this be done?

.... 1

GENERAL PHYSICS 2008   78   OFFICIAL SQA PAST PAPERS

DO NOT
WRITE IN
THIS
MARGIN

K&U   PS

Marks

19. Read the following passage about a space mission to the moons of Jupiter.

The spacecraft will use a new kind of engine called an ion drive. The ion drive will propel the spacecraft away from Earth on its journey to the moons of Jupiter, although for much of the journey the engine will be switched off.

The spacecraft will first visit the moon Callisto.

Callisto is only slightly smaller than the planet Mercury. Next, the spacecraft will visit Ganymede, the largest moon in the Solar System, before travelling on to Europa.

The radiation around Europa is so intense that the spacecraft will not be able to operate for long before becoming damaged beyond repair.

The spacecraft will eventually burn up in the atmosphere of Jupiter.

(a) (i) Name one object, **mentioned in the passage**, which orbits a planet.

....   1

(ii) State what is meant by the term Solar System.

....   1

(b) (i) The ion drive engine exerts a backward force on small particles called ions.
Explain how the ion drive engine is propelled forwards.

....   1

(ii) The mass of the spacecraft is 1200 kilograms and the thrust produced by the engine is 3 newtons.
Calculate the maximum acceleration produced by the ion drive engine.

Space for working and answer

2

(c) State why the ion drive engine need not be kept on for most of the journey from Earth to Jupiter.

....   1

Marks

20. (*a*) A ray of green light strikes a triangular prism as shown.

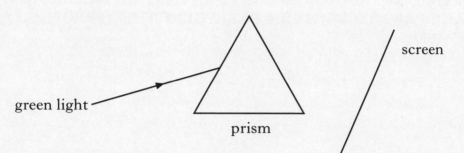

green light

prism

screen

(i) Complete the diagram to show the path of the ray of green light as it passes through the prism and on to the screen.

1

(ii) The green light is now replaced by white light.
Describe what is now observed on the screen.

.... 1

(iii) State **one** colour which has a longer wavelength than green light.

.... 1

(*b*) Light from a star produces a line spectrum.
What information is obtained about the star from this spectrum?

.... 1

[*END OF QUESTION PAPER*]

YOU MAY USE THE SPACE ON THIS PAGE TO REWRITE ANY ANSWER
YOU HAVE DECIDED TO CHANGE IN THE MAIN PART OF THE ANSWER
BOOKLET. TAKE CARE TO WRITE IN CAREFULLY THE APPROPRIATE
QUESTION NUMBER.

DO NOT
WRITE IN
THIS
MARGIN

K&U | PS

YOU MAY USE THE SPACE ON THIS PAGE TO REWRITE ANY ANSWER YOU HAVE DECIDED TO CHANGE IN THE MAIN PART OF THE ANSWER BOOKLET. TAKE CARE TO WRITE IN CAREFULLY THE APPROPRIATE QUESTION NUMBER.

YOU MAY USE THE SPACE ON THIS PAGE TO REWRITE ANY ANSWER YOU HAVE DECIDED TO CHANGE IN THE MAIN PART OF THE ANSWER BOOKLET. TAKE CARE TO WRITE IN CAREFULLY THE APPROPRIATE QUESTION NUMBER.

YOU MAY USE THE SPACE ON THIS PAGE TO REWRITE ANY ANSWER YOU HAVE DECIDED TO CHANGE IN THE MAIN PART OF THE ANSWER BOOKLET. TAKE CARE TO WRITE IN CAREFULLY THE APPROPRIATE QUESTION NUMBER.

[BLANK PAGE]

STANDARD GRADE | GENERAL

2009

[BLANK PAGE]

FOR OFFICIAL USE

G

K&U   PS

3220/401

NATIONAL
QUALIFICATIONS
2009

TUESDAY, 26 MAY
9.00 AM – 10.30 AM

PHYSICS
STANDARD GRADE
General Level

Fill in these boxes and read what is printed below.

Full name of centre

Town

Forename(s)

Surname

Date of birth
Day   Month   Year   Scottish candidate number

Number of seat

Reference may be made to the Physics Data Booklet.

1 All questions should be answered.

2 The questions may be answered in any order but all answers must be written clearly and legibly in this book.

3 For questions 1–6, write down, in the space provided, the letter corresponding to the answer you think is correct. There is only **one** correct answer.

4 For questions 7–20, write your answer where indicated by the question or in the space provided after the question.

5 If you change your mind about your answer you may score it out and replace it in the space provided at the end of the answer book.

6 If you use the additional space at the end of the answer book for answering any questions, you **must** write the correct question number beside each answer.

7 Before leaving the examination room you must give this book to the invigilator. If you do not, you may lose all the marks for this paper.

Use **blue** or **black ink**. Pencil may be used for graphs and diagrams only.

SA 3220/401 6/20420

K&U	PS

Marks

1. What is the frequency of a wave, if 20 crests pass a point in two seconds?

   A   0·1 hertz

   B   2   hertz

   C   10 hertz

   D   20 hertz

   E   40 hertz

   Answer [C]   1

2. How long does a geostationary satellite take to orbit the Earth?

   A   1 hour

   B   1 day

   C   1 week

   D   1 month

   E   1 year

   Answer [B]   1

3. Which of the following will **not allow** the transmission of sound waves?

   A   Brick

   B   Vacuum

   C   Water

   D   Air

   E   Wood

   Answer [A] B   1

4. Which of the following statements is **always** true about the structure of the atom?

   A   It has more electrons than protons. × — ion

   B   It has more protons than neutrons. ×

   C   It has an equal number of protons and electrons. .

   D   It has more neutrons than protons. ✓

   E   It has an equal number of neutrons and electrons. ✓

   Answer [A] C   1

Marks

5. Which of the following is a digital output device?

A   Solenoid

B   Loudspeaker

C   Motor

D   Lamp

E   Microphone

Answer B A   **1**

6. In which of the following would a voltage **not** be induced in a coil of wire?

A   Rotating the coil of wire near to a magnet

B   Rotating a magnet near to the coil of wire

C   Holding a magnet stationary within the coil of wire

D   Moving a magnet in and out of the coil of wire

E   Moving the coil of wire between the poles of a magnet

Answer C   **1**

[Turn over

Marks

7. A student listens to his radio using headphones.

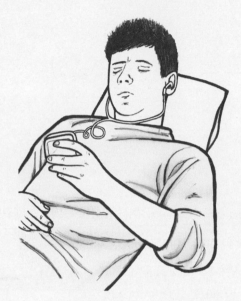

(*a*) State the main energy transformation that takes place in the headphones.

Electrical → Sound

1

The table shows the frequencies for different radio stations.

Radio Station	Frequency (mega hertz)
Forth 1	97·3
Real Radio	101·0
Radio Borders	103·1
Isles	103·0
Central Scotland FM	103·1
Radio Scotland	95·0

(*b*) Explain why the radio stations Radio Borders and Central Scotland FM are allowed to transmit at the same frequency.

because they are at different parts of the country therefore radios from Central Scotland would not pick up the signal from radio Borders

1

Marks

7. (continued)

(*c*) The block diagram shows some of the main parts of a radio receiver.

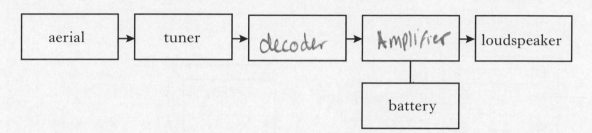

(i) Complete the block diagram by filling in the missing labels. **1**

(ii) What is the purpose of the tuner? ~select a specific frequency~

...to...pick...out...one...signal...from...the...main **1**
recieved.

[Turn over

Marks

8. An experiment is set up to investigate sound waves.

   A signal generator is connected to a loudspeaker.

   The signal generator has a frequency control and an amplitude control.

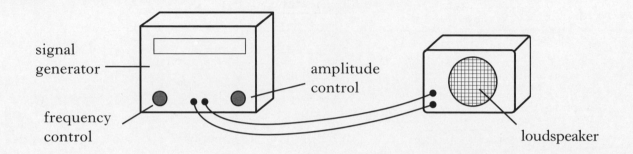

signal generator

amplitude control

frequency control

loudspeaker

(*a*) Complete the sentence below by circling the correct answer.

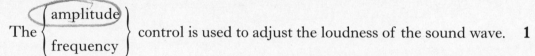

The $\left\{\begin{array}{c}\text{amplitude}\\\text{frequency}\end{array}\right\}$ control is used to adjust the loudness of the sound wave. **1**

(*b*) The controls of the signal generator are set up to produce a sound wave from the loudspeaker.

   An oscilloscope is now connected across the loudspeaker.

   The oscilloscope trace is shown in Figure 1.

   Complete Figure 2 to show the trace obtained when the frequency is **doubled**, but the amplitude remains unchanged.

   The oscilloscope controls are unchanged.

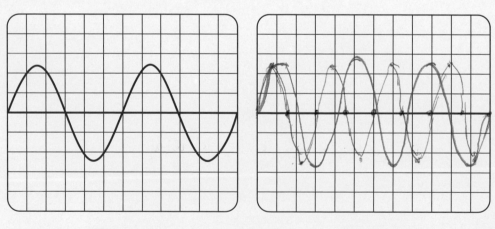

Figure 1   Figure 2   **2**

Marks

9. A design engineer uses three ammeters to measure the current, in amperes, at various points in the circuit of a model-sized electrical fan heater.

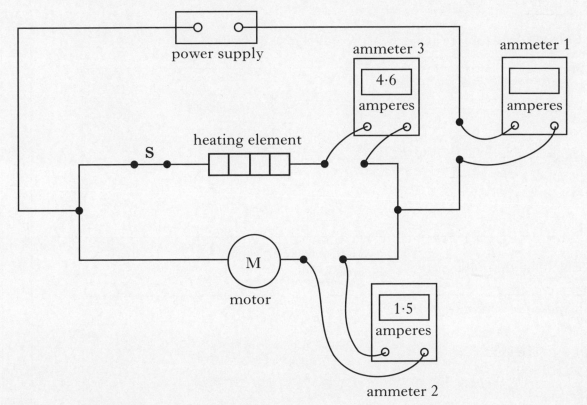

(a) Calculate the reading on ammeter 1.

> *Space for working and answer*
>
> I = 4.6 + 1.5 = 6.1 A

1

(b) What happens to the reading on ammeter 1 when switch **S** is opened?

....the current is broken so it is 1.5A.....................................

1

(c) The full size mains fan heater has a rating plate for UK supply stating its operating voltage and frequency.

Complete parts (i) and (ii) below by circling the correct answers.

(i) The voltage is $\left\{ \begin{array}{c} 110 \\ 230 \\ 325 \end{array} \right\}$ volts $\left\{ \begin{array}{c} a.c. \\ d.c. \end{array} \right\}$.

2

(ii) The mains frequency is $\left\{ \begin{array}{c} 50 \\ 60 \\ 115 \end{array} \right\}$ hertz.

1

Marks

10. Party lights consist of 16 identical light bulbs connected in (series.)

They operate from a 24 volt power supply. The current in the circuit is 1·25 amperes. V_T

(a) Calculate the <u>total resistance</u> of the bulbs in the circuit.

> *Space for working and answer*
>
> Given- I = 1·25A   Solution - R = $\frac{V}{I}$
>
>   V = 24v   R = $\frac{24}{1·25}$
>
> find - R
>
> equation - R = $\frac{V}{I}$ R = 19·2 Ω

2

2

(b) Calculate the <u>voltage</u> across each light bulb.

> *Space for working and answer* $V_b = I_b R_b$
>
> Given - I = 1·25
>
> $V_b = \frac{V_T}{16} = \frac{24}{16} = \boxed{1·5 V}$

1

0

(c) A fault occurs in the circuit and a continuity tester is needed to find the fault. The circuit diagram for the continuity tester is shown.

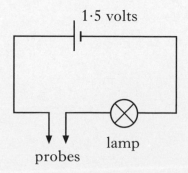

1·5 volts

probes   lamp

(i) Describe how the continuity tester could be tested to make sure that it is working.

Connect the tester to the probes and see if the lamp works, If so, there is no fault.

1

1

(ii) The continuity tester is found to be faulty.

State one possible reason why it is not working.

The voltage may be to low to power the tester and the lamp.

1

1

Marks

10. (continued)

(*d*) Conventional filament lamps are now being replaced by discharge tubes.

filament lamp

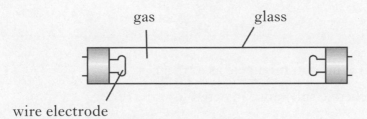

discharge tube

(i) State where the energy transformation occurs in:

(A) the filament lamp;

In the filament 1

(B) the discharge tube.

                    gas   in the tube
in the .... air around the wire 1

(ii) State why discharge tubes are replacing conventional filament lamps.

                    more
they are economic (weak) 1

more efficient

[Turn over

Marks

11. The electromagnetic spectrum is shown below.

radio & tv	microwaves	infrared	visible light	ultraviolet	X-rays	gamma rays

electromagnetic spectrum

Different types of waves in the spectrum are used in medicine.

(*a*) What property do all electromagnetic waves have in common?

the all have the same velocity   **1**

(*b*) Describe **one** use of X-rays in medicine.

to dectect broken bones   **1**

(*c*) Gamma radiation is used in medicine as a tracer.

A tracer is a radioactive substance injected into the body.

The gamma radiation then given off from the body is monitored.

(i) Explain why gamma radiation is used rather than alpha or beta radiation.

because only gamma can pass through the human body   **1**

(ii) What is the unit for the activity of the gamma radiation?

KBq   Bq   **1**

(*d*) Light can be produced by lasers.

Describe the use of the laser in **one** application of medicine.

bloodless operations (surgery)

1

K&U	PS

Marks

11. **(continued)**

(*e*) A student sets up the following experiment to compare how two different brands of sunglasses protect from ultraviolet radiation.

The student uses beads which change colour when exposed to ultraviolet radiation.

The student covers one set of beads with a lens from brand A and another with a lens from brand B.

The ultraviolet lamp is switched on for 30 minutes.

The apparatus is set up as shown.

ultraviolet lamp

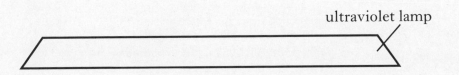

lens from brand A   lens from brand B

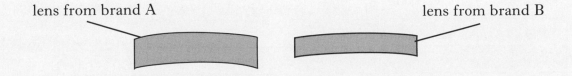

beads

beads

(i) Give **one** reason why this test is not a fair one.

.....because the lenses are diffent sizes..............   1

(ii) Why can exposure to ultraviolet radiation be harmful to humans?

.....because it Can Cause Skin Cancer..............   1

damage healthy cells

[Turn over

DO NOT
WRITE IN
THIS
MARGIN

K&U | PS

Marks

12. An orchestra uses many different musical instruments.

The table lists the lowest and highest sound frequencies for some of these instruments.

Musical Instrument	Lowest Frequency (hertz)	Highest Frequency (hertz)
Acoustic Guitar	73	1174
Piano	28	4186
Flute	261	2637
Trumpet	165	1046
Violin	196	3520
Cello	65	660
Piccolo	523	4000

(a) (i) Which instrument in the table produces the longest wavelength?

........piano............... $V = \lambda f$ **1**

(ii) Calculate the wavelength for the lowest frequency of a piccolo.

(The speed of sound in air is 340 metres per second.)

Space for working and answer

Given – V = 340 m/s
     – F = 523 hz

equation – V = fλ

λ = r/f

Solution –
$\lambda = \frac{340}{523}$

$\lambda = 0.65\ m$ **2**

(b) During one concert performance the sound level was measured.

State the unit of sound level measurement.

..........kBq... Dacibel   dB **1**

Marks

K&U	PS

13. A radio controlled model fire engine receives signals from a control unit.

One of the control functions operates a siren on the fire engine.

(a) State a suitable output device for the siren.

.... Loudspeaker 1

(b) The fire engine contains an electronic system to control the siren.

The signals at various parts of the system are displayed on oscilloscope screens.

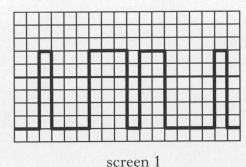

screen 1

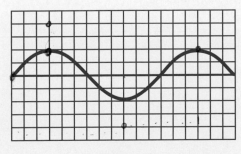

screen 2

    (i) Which screen shows a digital signal?

.... Screen 1 1

    (ii) The signal shown on screen 2 is now amplified.

The oscilloscope settings are unchanged.

Draw the amplified signal in the box below.

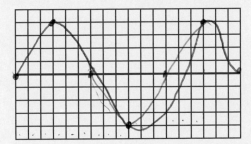

2

Marks

14. A pedestrian crossing at a set of traffic lights has an electronic control system to operate the "green man" light. Part of the system is shown.

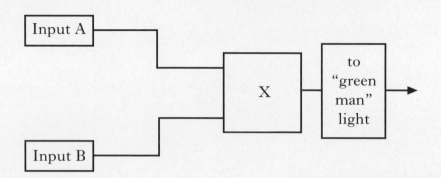

Input A is from the traffic lights and gives a logic 1 when the red light only is on, and a logic 0 at other times.

Input B is operated by pedestrians when they want to cross.

(*a*) State a suitable input device to be used by the pedestrians to activate the "green man" light.

............Push Switch...   1   /

(*b*) The "green man" light comes on when the red traffic light, only, is on and the crossing is operated by a pedestrian. What type of logic gate should be used at position X?

............And...   1   /

(*c*) The "green man" light consists of a number of LEDs.

   (i) Draw the symbol for an LED.

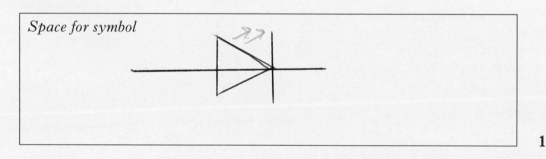

Space for symbol

1   0

   (ii) Why does each LED need a series resistor?

......So the current doesn't get to high...........   1   /
and damage the LED

DO NOT WRITE IN THIS MARGIN

K&U	PS

Marks

14. (continued)

(*d*) The "green man" light has to stay on long enough for the pedestrian to cross.

This crossing has a display to show pedestrians the number of seconds the "green man" light will remain on.

State an output device that could be used to display this time.

Seven Segment display **1**

[Turn over

Marks

15. An indoor kart track hosts a racing competition.

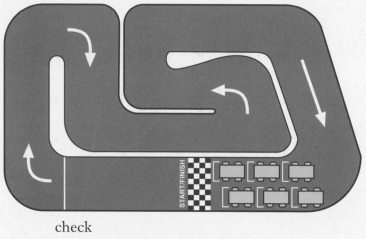

check
point X

(*a*) Describe how to find the average speed of a kart for one complete lap of
the track.

$V_{av} = \frac{d}{t}$ ✓

You must state the measurements that are made and how they are used.

......find the total distance using a trundle......

...wheel the record the time of 1 kart going......

......round the track using a stopwatch......   3

(*b*) The speed of a kart and driver is recorded from the start of the race.

The kart starts from rest and accelerates uniformly until it reaches check
point X. Its speed at X is 12 metres per second.

The time taken to reach X is 4 seconds.

(i) Draw a speed-time graph for the motion of the kart from the start
until it reaches check point X.

Units and numerical values must be shown on both axes.

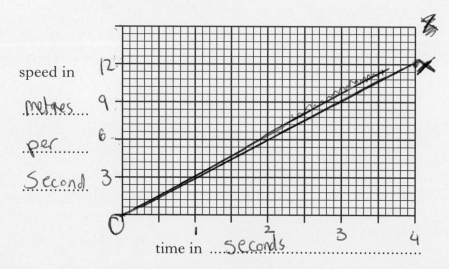

speed in

metres

per

Second

time in ...seconds...   3

Marks

15. **(b)** **(continued)**

(ii) Calculate the acceleration of the kart between the start and check point X.

> *Space for working and answer*
>
> Given $\quad v = 12$
> $\qquad\qquad u = 0$
> $\qquad\qquad t = 4$
>
> equation $- a = \dfrac{v - u}{t}$
>
> Solution $- a = \dfrac{v - u}{t}$
>
> $\qquad\qquad a = \dfrac{12 - 0}{4}$
>
> $\qquad\qquad a = 3 \ m/s^2$

2

2

(c) Some spectators at the race track are finding it difficult to see the race.

One spectator uses a periscope. A periscope can be made from a cardboard tube with two plane mirrors as shown.

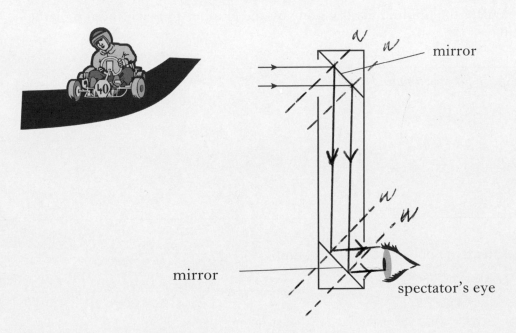

mirror

mirror

spectator's eye

Complete the diagram to show how the rays of light travel through the periscope to the spectator's eye.

1

1

[Turn over

DO NOT WRITE IN THIS MARGIN

K&U | PS

Marks

16. A climber of weight 550 newtons takes 40 seconds to reach the top of a 20 metre high climbing wall.

(a) What is the minimum upward force she exerts while climbing the wall?

.... 550 N 1   1

(b) Calculate the minimum work done by the climber to reach the top of the wall.

> Space for working and answer
>
> $E_W = Fd = 550 \times 20 = 11000 \text{ J}$

2   0

(c) Calculate her power during this climb. $P = \dfrac{E}{t} = \dfrac{11000}{40} = 275$

> Space for working and answer
>
> Given — t = 40s   Speed
> d = 20m
>
> equation - d = vt
> v = $\frac{d}{t}$
>
> Solution V = $\frac{20}{40}$ V = 0·5m/s
>
> Given - v = 0·5m/s
> - m = 550n   Power
>
> equation - P = mv   Wrong physics
>
> Solution - P = mv
> P = 550 × 0·5
> P = 275 W

2   0

(d) Explain why the climber uses chalk on her hands as she climbs the wall.

.... to get a better grip 1   1

DO NOT
WRITE IN
THIS
MARGIN

K&U | PS

Marks

17. A house is designed to conserve as much energy as possible.

(*a*) Heat energy can be lost from the house by a variety of means. Insulation is used to reduce heat loss.

Match the correct type of insulation given in the word bank with each type of heat loss.

Use each answer once only.

foil-backed plasterboard	double glazing	loft insulation

Type of heat loss	Correct insulation
Conduction	double glazing
Convection	loft insulation
Radiation	foil backed plasterboard

2

2

The temperature in the house is kept at a constant value while the temperature outside changes.

The graph shows the temperature inside the house and the temperature outside the house over a 24 hour period.

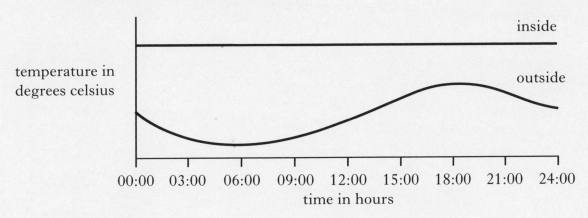

(*b*) Write down the time at which heat loss from the house is greatest.

06:00

1

1

Marks

18. Increasing the amount of electricity generated from renewable sources is important for the future of our country.

(*a*) At present, fossil fuels are the main source of energy.

State **one** problem with this source of energy.

...........It...is...a...finite...Sourc............................... 1

(*b*) The bar chart shows the main energy sources used in Scotland.

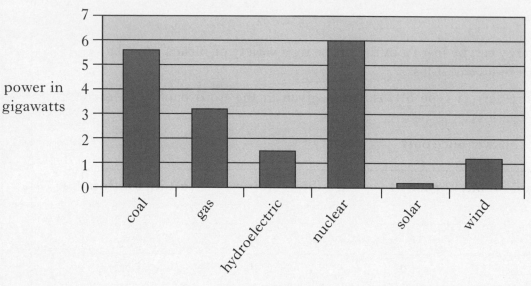

Use the names of the energy sources in the bar chart to complete the table.

Renewable	*Non-renewable*
hydro electric Wind Solar	Nuclear gas Coal

2

DO NOT
WRITE IN
THIS
MARGIN

K&U | PS

Marks

18. (continued)

(*c*) A nuclear power station with a power output of 1·5 gigawatts could be replaced by pumped hydroelectric power stations.

(i) Some of the stages in a nuclear power station are shown.

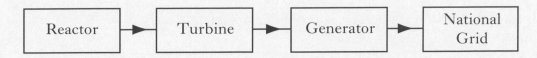

Reactor → Turbine → Generator → National Grid

At what stage is the main energy transformation:

(A) kinetic → electrical;

.......Generator.. 1

(B) nuclear → heat?

.......reactor.. 1

A pumped hydroelectric power station produces 0·25 gigawatts of power.

(ii) Give **one** advantage of a pumped hydroelectric station over a normal hydroelectric station.

.......the water can be reused rather than.......

.......be wasted.. 1

(iii) How many pumped hydroelectric stations would be needed to replace the nuclear power station?

Space for working and answer

$\dfrac{1.5}{.25}$

1

[Turn over

Marks

19. (a) State an optical device that can split white light into different colours.

triangular prism

1

(b) Astronomers can use the peak wavelength of light emitted by stars to provide information about their temperature. The peak wavelength corresponds to a particular colour.

Information about three stars is given in the table.

Star	Colour of peak wavelength in visible spectrum
Rigel	Blue
Betelgeuse	Red
Sun	Green

The shorter the peak wavelength, the hotter the star is.

(i) Which star is hottest?

Rigel

1

(ii) Is the sun hotter, colder or the same temperature as Betelgeuse?

hotter

1

(c) Telescopes can detect visible light waves.

Name **one** other type of wave that can be detected using a telescope.

radio

1

19. **(continued)**

(*d*) The planet Venus is often seen in the evening and morning close to the horizon.

Draw light rays on the diagram to show how observers on Earth are able to see Venus.

You must put arrows on the rays to show their direction.

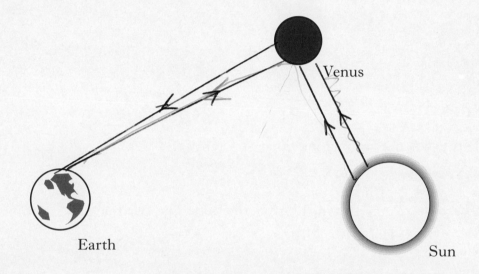

Venus

Earth

Sun

Marks

2

[Turn over

Marks

20. Astronomers study space.

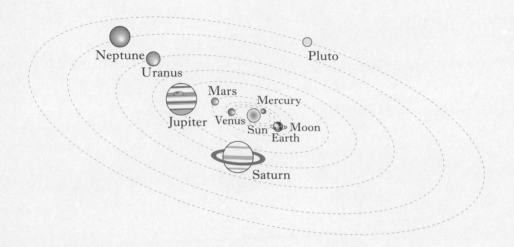

Complete the sentences by circling the correct answers.

(*a*) The Earth is a $\left\{ \begin{array}{l} \text{planet} \\ \text{moon} \\ \text{star} \end{array} \right\}$ which orbits the Sun. The Earth has one natural

satellite called the $\left\{ \begin{array}{l} \text{International Space station} \\ \text{Hubble telescope} \\ \text{Moon} \end{array} \right\}$.   **1**

(*b*) The Sun is at the centre of our $\left\{ \begin{array}{l} \text{solar system} \\ \text{universe} \\ \text{galaxy} \end{array} \right\}$. Light from the Sun takes

about $\left\{ \begin{array}{l} \text{8 seconds} \\ \text{4·3 years} \\ \text{8 minutes} \end{array} \right\}$ to travel to the Earth.   **1**

(*c*) The nearest star to the Earth is $\left\{ \begin{array}{l} \text{Sirius} \\ \text{Mars} \\ \text{the Sun} \end{array} \right\}$.

All of space is known as the $\left\{ \begin{array}{l} \text{Milky Way} \\ \text{solar system} \\ \text{universe} \end{array} \right\}$.   **1**

[*END OF QUESTION PAPER*]

DO NOT WRITE IN THIS MARGIN

K&U | PS

ADDITIONAL SPACE FOR ANSWERS

Make sure you write the correct question number beside each answer.

K&U | PS

ADDITIONAL SPACE FOR ANSWERS

Make sure you write the correct question number beside each answer.

DO NOT
WRITE IN
THIS
MARGIN

K&U   PS

ADDITIONAL SPACE FOR ANSWERS

Make sure you write the correct question number beside each answer.

K&U   PS

ADDITIONAL SPACE FOR ANSWERS

Make sure you write the correct question number beside each answer.

[BLANK PAGE]

[BLANK PAGE]